Company Diagnosis:

Mission

To continually provide our members with quality goods and services at the lowest possible prices.

Objectives

We will exceed 10% net sales by getting over 125 of warehouses to exceed 200 million in sales and by offering our members great products and services at the lowest possible prices.

We will increase membership fees by over 10% by raising our yearly subscription fees and by maintaining our strong renewal rates, getting new-signups at new locations and by penetrating additional Executive membership programs.

We will drive down our (SG&A) expenses by 15 percentage points. We will achieve this by making improvements to overall operating costs in warehouses mainly around payroll and the leveraging of operating expenses with strong sales results.

Corporate Strategy

Our strategy is to provide our members with a broad range of high quality merchandise at prices consistently lower than they can obtain elsewhere. We seek to limit specific items in each product line to fast-selling models, sizes, and colors. Therefore, we carry an average of approximately 3,300 to 3,800 active stock keeping units (SKUs) per warehouse in our core warehouse business, as opposed to a significantly higher number of SKUs at discount retailers, supermarkets, and supercenters. Many consumable products are offered for sale in case, carton, or multiple-pack quantities only.

Key Information

Membership Policy:
Our membership format is designed to reinforce member loyalty and provide a continuing source of membership fee revenue. Members can utilize their membership at any Costco warehouse location in any country. We have two primary types of members: Business and Gold Star (individual). Our member renewal rate was approximately 89.7% in the U.S. and Canada, and approximately 86.4% on a worldwide basis in 2012, consistent with recent years.

Warehouses and Headquarters:
Our typical warehouse format averages approximately 143,000 square feet; newer units tend to be slightly larger. Floor plans are designed for economy and efficiency in the use of selling space, the handling of merchandise, and the control of inventory. Because shoppers are attracted principally by the quality of merchandise and the availability of low prices, our warehouses are not elaborate facilities. By strictly controlling the entrances and exits of our warehouses and using a membership format, we have limited inventory losses (shrinkage) to amounts well below those of typical discount retail operations.

At the end of 2012, our warehouses contained approximately 86.9 million square feet of operating floor space: 63.7 million in the U.S.; 11.2 million in Canada; and 12.0 million in other international locations.

Our executive offices are located in Issaquah, Washington and occupy approximately 590,000 square feet. We operate eight regional offices in the U.S., two regional offices in Canada and six regional offices internationally, containing approximately 423,000 square feet. Additionally, we operate regional cross-docking facilities (depots) for the consolidation and distribution of most merchandise shipments to the warehouses, and various processing, packaging, and other facilities to support ancillary and other businesses. We operate 12 depots in the U.S., four in Canada and five internationally, consisting of approximately 8.7 million square feet.

Our primary requirement for capital is the financing of land, buildings, and equipment costs for new and remodeled warehouses. To a lesser extent, capital is required for initial warehouse operations and working capital. While there can be no assurance that current expectations will be realized and plans are subject to change upon further review, it is our current intention to spend approximately $1,800 to $2,000 during fiscal 2013 for real estate, construction, remodeling, equipment for warehouses and related operations, and the modernization of our information systems and related activities. These expenditures are expected to be financed with a combination of cash provided from operations and existing cash and cash equivalents and short-term investments.

Online:
Our online businesses at costco.com in the U.S. and costco.ca in Canada, provide our members additional products generally not found in our warehouses, in addition to services such as digital photo processing, pharmacy, travel, and membership services.

52-Week Stock Performance

Costco's stock has shown consistent growth within the last 52 weeks. As of November 21, 2014, Costco's stock price closed at $139.72; which is $1.58 less than their highest historical price per share of $140.83.

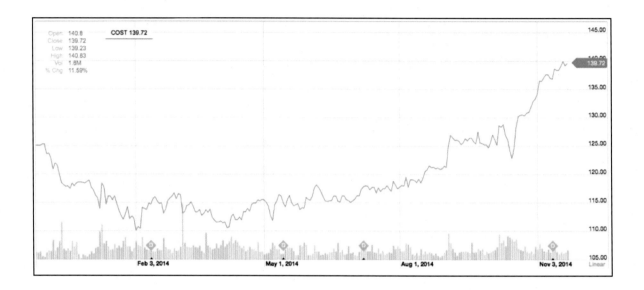

10-Year Comparative Stock Performance

Since 2011, Costco has seen tremendous growth in the stock market and outperformed their competition. As of November 21, 2014 Costco and its competitors are trading at the following prices:

- Costco - $139.31
- Carrefour - $25.30
- Target - $71.51
- Walmart - $64.65

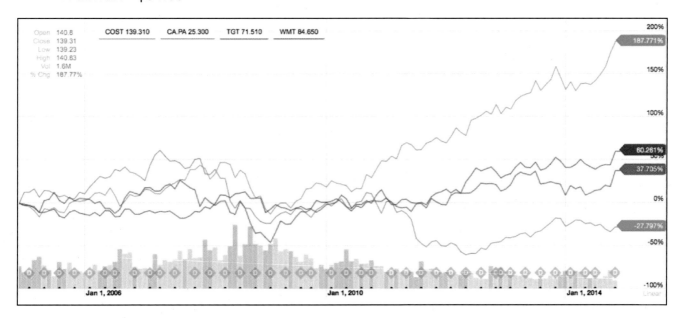

Legend:
Costco – Blue
Carrefour SA – Green
Target – Pink
Walmart - Red

Policies:

A. **Diversity:** Diversity in our employee base as well as our Supplier base is an important aspect of our business; by developing and maintaining partnerships with certified minority and women owned businesses, we are able to explore new ideas and maintain a fresh approach to our business, while positively affecting the economic development in the communities where we do business.

B. **Ethical Standards/Code of Conduct:**
   a. Obey the law.
   b. Take care of our members
   c. Take care of our employees
   d. Respect suppliers
   e. Reward our shareholders
   f. Comply with all laws and other legal requirements.
   g. Respect all public officials and their positions.
   h. Comply with safety and security standards for all products sold.
   i. Alert management if we observe illegal workplace misconduct by other employees.
   j. Exceed ecological standards required in every community where we do business.
   k. Comply with all applicable wage and hour laws.
   l. Comply with all applicable antitrust laws.
   m. Conduct business in and with foreign countries in a manner that is legal and proper under
   n. United States and foreign laws.
   o. Not offer or give any form of bribe or kickback or other thing of value to any person or pay to obtain or expedite government action or otherwise act in violation of the Foreign Corrupt Practices Act or the laws of other countries.
   p. Not request or receive any bribe or kickback.
   q. Promote fair, accurate, timely, and understandable disclosure in reports filed with the Securities and Exchange Commission and in other public communications by the Company.

C. **Suppliers:** Our Suppliers are our partners in business and for us to prosper as a company they must prosper with us. To that end, we strive to:

   a. Treat all suppliers and their representatives as we would expect to be treated if visiting their places of business.

b. Honor all commitments.

c. Protect all suppliers' property assigned to Costco as though it were our own.

d. Not accept gratuities of any kind from a supplier.

D. **Human Resources:** Our employees are our most important asset. We believe we have the very best employees in the warehouse club industry, and we are committed to providing them with rewarding challenges and ample opportunities for personal and career growth. We pledge to provide our employees with:

a. Competitive wages

b. Great benefits

c. A safe and healthy work environment

d. Challenging and fun work

e. Career opportunities

f. An atmosphere free from harassment or discrimination

g. An Open Door Policy that allows access to ascending levels of management to resolve issues

h. Opportunities to give back to their communities through volunteerism and fund-raising

E. **Career Philosophy:**

a. Costco is committed to promoting from within the Company. The majority of our current management team members (including Warehouse, Merchandise, Administrative, Membership, Front End and Receiving Managers) are "home grown."

b. Our growth plans remain very aggressive and our need for qualified, experienced employees to fill supervisory and management positions remains great.

c. Today we have Location Managers and Vice Presidents who were once Stockers and Callers or who started in clerical positions for Costco. We believe that Costco's future executive officers are currently working in our warehouses, depots and buying offices, as well as in our Home Office.

Strategic Managers and Board:

A. Senior Level Executives

Jeffrey H. Brotman
Board: Executive Board
Job Title: Chairman of the Board Since: 1994
Age: 71

Richard A. Galanti
Board: Executive Board
Job Title: Executive Vice President and Chief Financial Officer
Since: 1993
Age: 57

W. Craig Jelinek
Board: Non Executive Board
Job Title: President and Chief Executive Officer Since: 2012
Age: 61

Hamilton E. James
Board: Non Executive Board
Job Title: Director
Since: 2005
Age: 62

Benjamin S. Carson, Sr.
Board: Non Executive Board
Job Title: Director
Since: 1999
Age: 62

Susan L. Decker
Board: Non Executive Board
Job Title: Director
Since: 2004
Age: 51

Daniel J. Evans
Board: Non Executive Board
Job Title: Director
Since: 2003 Age: 88

William H. Gates, Sr.
Board: Non Executive Board
Job Title: Director
Since: 2003
Age: 88

Richard M. Libenson
Board: Non Executive Board
Job Title: Director
Since: 1993
Age: 71

John W. Meisenbach
Board: Non Executive Board
Job Title: Director
Since: 1983
Age: 77

Charles T. Munger
Board: Non Executive Board
Job Title: Director
Since: 1997
Age: 89

Jeffrey S. Raikes
Board: Non Executive Board
Job Title: Director
Since: 2008
Age: 55

Jill S. Ruckelshaus
Board: Non Executive Board Job Title: Director
Since: 1996
Age: 76

James D. Sinegal
Board: Non Executive Board
Job Title: Director
Since: 1983
Age: 77

Franz Lazarus
Board: Senior Management
Job Title: Executive Vice President, Administration and Human
Resources Age: 66

John McKay
Board: Senior Management
Job Title: Executive Vice President and Chief Operating Officer,
Northern Division and Midwest Region
Age: 56

Paul G. Moulton Board: Senior Management Job Title: Executive Vice President, Information Systems Age: 62	
James P. Murphy Board: Senior Management Job Title: Executive Vice President, International Age: 60	
Joseph P. Portera Board: Senior Management Job Title: Executive Vice President and Chief Operating Officer, Eastern and Canadian Divisions Age: 61	
Douglas W. Schutt Board: Senior Management Job Title: Executive Vice President and Chief Operating Officer, Merchandising Age: 54	
Timothy L. Rose Board: Senior Management Job Title: Executive Vice President, Costco Wholesale Industries Age: 61	

B. Corporate Governance:

    a. Responsibilities: The business and affairs of the Company shall be managed under the direction of the Board. A director is expected to spend the time and effort necessary to properly discharge such director's responsibilities. Accordingly, a director is expected to regularly attend meetings of the Board and committees on which such director sits, and to review prior to meetings material distributed in advance. A director who is unable to attend a meeting (which will unavoidably occur on occasion) is expected to notify the Chairman of the Board or the Chairman of the appropriate committee in advance of such meeting.

    b. Board Committees:

Audit Committee:

The Costco Wholesale Corporation Audit Committee is nominated and elected by the Board of Directors each year at the meeting of the Board of Directors held in conjunction with the Company's Annual Meeting of Shareholders. The Audit Committee will be composed of from three to five directors, each of whom must in the judgment of the Board be "independent" as defined by the rules of the Securities and Exchange Commission ("SEC"). At least one member of the Committee shall in the judgment of the Board be an "audit committee financial expert" as defined by the SEC. Each member of the Committee shall meet the financial literacy and other applicable requirements of the NASDAQ Stock Market listing standards. Other personnel may attend meetings of the Committee at the invitation of the Committee or its Chairman.

Compensation Committee:

The Compensation Committee will be comprised of at least two members of the Board. Committee members will be elected by and serve at the discretion of the Board. Unless a chair is elected by the Board, the members of the Committee may designate a chair by vote of the Committee.

Each member of the Committee will be: (1) "independent" as defined under applicable Nasdaq (or applicable stock exchange) rules (except as otherwise permitted under such rules); (2) a "non-employee director" under Rule 16b-3(b)(3)(i) promulgated under the Securities Exchange Act of 1934; and (3) as an "outside director" under the rules promulgated under section 162(m) of the Internal Revenue Code of 1986.

In the event that the Committee has more than two members and one or more members of the Committee are absent from a meeting of the Committee or being present at a meeting recuse themselves from an action taken, the remaining members of the Committee (provided there are at least two such members) acting unanimously shall have the power to take any necessary action. No action of the Committee shall be valid unless taken pursuant to a resolution adopted and approved by at least two members of the Committee. Except with respect to matters relating to compensation of the Chief Executive Officer ("CEO"), with respect to which the Board delegates to the Committee exclusive authority during such period of time that the Committee is empanelled with at least two qualifying members as required above, the Board simultaneously reserves to itself all authority delegated hereunder to the Committee. This reservation of authority does not in any way limit the Committee's authority to act definitively on matters delegated to it. The Board reserves the right at any time to revoke or change the authority delegated in this charter.

Nominating and Governance Committee:

The purpose of the Nominating and Governance Committee (the "Committee") of the Board of Directors of Costco Wholesale Corporation (the "Company") is to identify and approve individuals qualified to serve as members of the Board of the Company, select director nominees for the next annual meeting of stockholders, evaluate the Board's performance, develop and recommend to the Board corporate governance guidelines, and provide oversight with respect to corporate governance and the compliance and ethics program.

The Committee shall be composed of three or more directors, as determined by the Board of Directors, each of whom shall meet the independence requirements required by law and the relevant stock exchange listing requirements.

c. **Director Compensation:**

Name	Job Title	Board	Compensation
Jeffrey H. Brotman	Chairman of the Board	Executive Board	$5,103,085.00
Richard A. Galanti	Executive Vice President and Chief Financial Officer	Executive Board	$3,146,925.00
W. Craig Jelinek	President and Chief Executive Officer	Non Executive Board	$5,385,475.00
Hamilton E. James	Director	Non Executive Board	$312,221.00
Benjamin S. Carson, Sr.	Director	Non Executive Board	$315,221.00
Susan L. Decker	Director	Non Executive Board	$315,221.00
Daniel J. Evans	Director	Non Executive Board	$323,221.00
William H. Gates, Sr.	Director	Non Executive Board	$316,221.00
Richard M. Libenson	Director	Non Executive Board	$639,274.00
John W. Meisenbach	Director	Non Executive Board	$312,221.00
Charles T. Munger	Director	Non Executive Board	$322,221.00
Jeffrey S. Raikes	Director	Non Executive Board	$312,221.00
Jill S. Ruckelshaus	Director	Non Executive Board	$318,221.00
James D. Sinegal	Director	Non Executive Board	$105,907.00

Generic Industry Type

Domestic Industry:

A. **Industry Definition:** NAICS- 45291: Warehouse Clubs and Supercenters. This industry comprises large stores that primarily retail a general line of grocery products, along with merchandise items (e.g. apparel and appliances). Warehouse clubs offer customers a wide selection of goods, often in bulk, at discounted prices, in exchange for a membership fee paid by each customer. Supercenters are large discount department stores that also sell perishable groceries. However, unlike warehouse clubs, supercenters do not have eligibility requirements for customers.

B. **Market Size and Growth Rate:** This industry is highly concentrated. The top two companies in the industry, Walmart and Costco, together account for 81.5% of industry revenue in 2014. Given the high level of industry concentration and substantial capital required to generate enough revenue to compete with the major players, IBISWorld expects concentration to remain high.

C. **Key Rivals & Market Share:** Walmart Stores, Inc - 64.4%; Costco Wholesale Corporation - 17.1%; Other - 18.5%

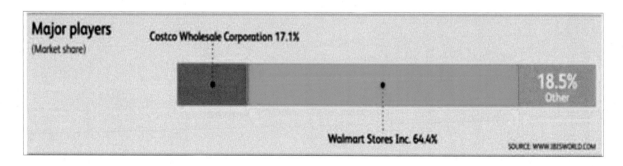

D. Scope of Competitive Rivalry:

Internal Competition: Price is the most important basis of competition in the industry. The recession put a premium on value over convenience and selection. Consumers expect low prices but maybe willing to pay more for larger economy sizes and a lower cost per serving. In a study 2012 by Nielsen, when asked how consumers would prefer manufacturers to address a price increase in raw materials, 38.0% stated that they would prefer to purchase larger sizes with lower per-serving or per-use costs. Consumers look for monetary value in their purchases, so some operators set their prices in conjunction with product strategies and marketing programs to remain competitive.

External Competition: The industry is also subject to external competition from a range of operators outside of the industry that supply a similar line of products. Each of the following industries supplies products that are also sold by club stores and supercenters, providing consumers with an alternative store from which to make their purchases. Some of the specialty retailers include: furniture stores, suppliers of new household, outdoor and office furniture; home furnishing stores, suppliers of new home furnishings; supermarkets that stock general lines of food products; hardware stores, suppliers of a general line of new hardware items, such as tools and builders' hardware; convenience stores; men's, women's and children's clothing stores; department stores; and dollar and variety stores.

External businesses generally compete on product range, brands offered, store design, location and especially price. The homogeneous goods offered and the saturated market means that many of these external competitors try to undercut each other in price.

E. **Concentration vs. Fragmentation:** This industry is highly concentrated. The top two companies in the industry, Walmart and Costco, together account for 81.5% of industry revenue in 2014. Given the high level of industry concentration and substantial capital required to generate enough revenue to compete with the major players, IBISWorld expects concentration to remain high.

F. **Number of Buyers:** Key Buying Industries include: Day Care in the US, Bed & Breakfast & Hostel Accommodations in the US, Hair and Nail Salons in the US, Civic, Social and Youth Organizations in the US, and Consumers in the US.

G. **Demand Determinants:** Demand is determined by disposable household income. However due to the diversity of products and values offered within the industry, downturns in the economy are less impactful. The chart below illustrates the major market segmentation.

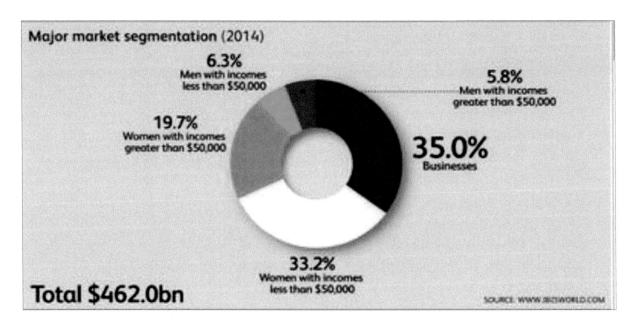

H. **Degree of Product Differentiation:** The Warehouse Industry provides a variety of goods and service which fall into five major segments as shown in the graph below:

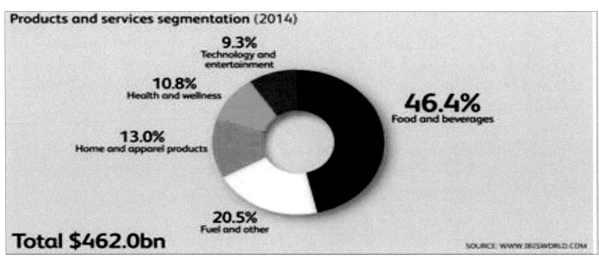

I. **Product Innovation:** The Warehouse Clubs and Supercenters industry provides a range of general merchandise, including: food and beverages; technology and entertainment; home and apparel; health and wellness; and fuel and other goods. Due to the recession and slow recovery that altered much of the retail landscape, the product market for the industry has undergone some changes as consumers have altered their spending patterns and industry operators have expanded their offerings. Increasingly, this industry provides a range of ancillary services, including gas stations, pharmacies and optical stores within store premises. Strong demand for one-stop shopping experiences has led to positive reaction to such services within warehouse clubs and supercenters; as such, this service segment as a share of revenue has increased slightly over the past five years. In 2014, this segment is estimated to account for 20.5% of total industry sales. Furthermore, this industry will continue to expand its private label consumer goods to compete with name brands. These private label goods generally offer comparable quality at discount pricing, while generating additional profit margins for the stores.

J. **Key Success Factors:**

   Loyal Customer Base: operators to insure consumer needs are met, especially stores that require paid memberships.

   Stock Control: control measures in place to restock popular items efficiently, dispose low-selling products and provide a sufficient product range.

   Product Range: should be competitive with competitors in and outside the industry.

   Competitors include but are not limited to: supermarkets, grocery stores, department stores, and furniture stores.

   Car Parking: due to large sizes of the stores, sufficient lot sizes must be included for parking and customer convenience.

   Economies of Scale: help industry participants lower the cost of doing business, passing the savings onto the consumers.

   Distribution Control: control privately owned distribution facilities or maintain strict agreements with distributors.

K. **Supply/Demand Conditions:** Consumers and businesses spend liberally on discretionary goods when the economic outlook is strong, unemployment is low and households and businesses have robust income. This leads to high demand for retail goods, including those sold at warehouse clubs and supercenters. While most retail industries typically struggle when the opposite conditions are occurring, the Warehouse Clubs and Supercenters industry remains resilient because it's discounted prices continue to attract households and businesses.

Such was the case during the recession, when disposable income marked its first decline in nearly two decades and industry revenue still grew 0.4% in 2009 .Retail sales are generally affected by shifts in household disposable incomes, consumer sentiment and business sentiment. Although these drivers also affect the Warehouse Clubs and Supercenters industry, the nature of the industry's value offerings makes it more resistant to downturns in the economy. Because club stores and supercenters retail a variety of general merchandise and groceries, they are susceptible to fluctuating demand for various types of goods. With convenience becoming more important to consumers, the variety of goods retailed at industry locations helps to boost sales. Time-strapped consumers prefer to shop where they can find all the products they need in one place. This trend has led to several industry players retailing gasoline at their stores. As gasoline price hikes make the stores' lower-priced gasoline more appealing to customers, sales of other goods within the stores generally rise because customers fulfill their other shopping needs as a matter of convenience.

L. **Analysis of Stage in Life Cycle:** The Warehouse Clubs and Supercenters industry is in the mature phase of its life cycle. In the 10 years to 2019, industry value added, a measure of the industry's contribution to the US economy, is forecast to increase at a rate of 3.9% per year on average. Comparatively, GDP is projected to rise at an annualized 2.7% over the same period. A slowdown in revenue growth and the moderation of profit; however, are expected to steady the industry's contribution to GDP. In addition, the number of industry enterprises has declined due to mergers and acquisitions during the five years to 2014, indicating the industry's mature state.

M. **Pace of Technological Change:** The use of technology has been limited to the implementation of point-of-sale systems and efficiencies in the supply chain, like radio frequency identification technology. While these systems have enabled operators to increase store efficiency and better manage inventory in the five years to 2014, further changes in technology are not expected in the next five years. Such slowdown of technology is also indicative of an industry in the mature stage of its life cycle. Technology and scale are at the core of the Warehouse Clubs and Supercenters industry's advantage over competing industries. Across the retail sector, stores that belong to chains tend to be more efficient than single-store retailers and chains tend to invest more in information technology. Improvements in point-of-sale (POS) equipment have brought greater efficiencies to merchandising, distribution, sales and stock markdowns. For example, inventory controlling radio frequency identification (RFID) stores more product information and can be scanned from a further distance than traditional bar codes. RFID provides real-time information on inventory, helping to reduce shrinkage problems and improve efficiency. Major player Walmart was a forerunner in rolling out RFID and has the ability to track all items throughout its supply chain. RFID tags can support a large amount of information about the product, and can be incorporated or attached to items. Increased knowledge and information allows retailers to minimize store shrinkage. However, cost remains a major obstacle to their implementation as manufacturers must absorb this cost.

N. **Vertical Integration:** Warehouse Clubs and Supercenters are partially vertically integrated with systems such as cross dock distribution. They have continued to focus on backward integration by producing their private label brands such as Kirkland.

O. Economies of Scale:

Economies of scale help industry participants lower the cost of doing business, which translates into lower prices for consumers. Warehouse clubs and supercenters are characterized by their large-scale operations, which give players in the industry an advantage in contracting with foreign suppliers to import at a lower average cost than applied to other retailers. The larger scale also allows operators to purchase goods in bulk, reducing the cost of distribution, stocking and labor per item sold. Opening stores close to each other has also allowed players to lower costs for distribution, training and advertising.

A successful business model for a warehouse club or supercenter depends on high volume of sales; therefore, low sales due to slow store traffic reduce efficiency and increase operating costs. Because companies stock only a few products in each category, merchandising misjudgments can disastrously affect sales. With thin margins, warehouse clubs depend on efficient operations to keep costs low, such as direct manufacturer shipments and cross-docking facilities to reduce distribution and storage costs. Companies must strike the proper balance between low inventory costs and potential lost sales.

P. **Barriers to Entry:** This industry has a high level of concentration since the 2 leaders make up 81.4% of the market share. Anyone looking to enter this space will be challenged heavily by the rulers of this space. The overall supremacy changes by region. It really comes down to economies of scale of where the operators plan open new locations. Another large thing to consider when entering this industry would be the heavy start-up costs. Those fees would include construction and development costs of between 5 and 7 million. Another cost would be acquiring the land. That could run between 3 and 5 million or in some areas much more. One would also need a heavy amount of capital to buy merchandise and bring in and train employees. The final thing to think about when entering this space would be around distribution networks. There is a very extensive reach of the industry, the aggressiveness of players to get manufactures products on shelves is very cutthroat. And the size of current occupants create challenges for those entering this territory.

Q. **Regulation/Deregulation:** Regulations around Warehouse clubs and Supercenters industry predominately revolve around pricing and size. Also, there are state that make operators administer the slightest markups to the specific goods such as tobacco products, alcoholic beverages and gasoline. Some states, counties and municipalities have executed or suggested laws to keep or narrow the operations or expansion plans of certain large retailers and warehouse club within their jurisdictions. Regulations around retail are driven primarily by the individual states. States have also executed their own antitrust laws to make sure the public is given the best prices, quality and choices. The laws that could have influence on credit programs awarded by retailers include the Federal Consumer Credit Protection Act (Truth in Lending), which distinguishes written disclosure of information relating to financing. Industry players are exposed to environmental regulations enforced by federal, state local authorities in regards to generation, handling, storage, transportation and disposal of waste and bio hazardous materials, likewise the sale and distribution of product. Finally, operators are also bound to regulation by the US Food and Drug Administration, the Department of Agriculture, the Occupational Health and Safety Administration and the Environment Protection agency.

R. **Globalization:** The bulk of this industry is US-owned and collects revenue from domestic operations. However, companies are beginning to spread their operations internationally. The power players within this space have enrolled in the global market. At this point, the bulk of revenue comes from domestic sales.

S. **Trends:** During the next five years, the industry will continue to grow, albeit at a slower rate, as retail giants such as Walmart and Target shift focus back to smaller, more conveniently sized stores, amid concerns that supercenters and warehouse clubs have reached a point of saturation. Still, improving disposable incomes, consumer sentiment and corporate profit, which are key drivers for the retail sector, will aid industry growth. In the five years to 2019, revenue is projected to increase at an average annual rate of 2.1% to $512.0 billion. Profit is also expected to grow slightly, reaching a projected 5.6% of revenue in 2019, up from an estimated 5.5% in 2014. Store expansion will be limited, however, as smaller operators continue consolidating, in order to compete with the players dominating market share. This trend, coupled with the shift toward smaller store formats, will likely limit the industry's long-term growth. During the recession, supercenters and clubs gained new customers as the economy weakened. While consumers and businesses are expected to adopt a positive outlook concerning the economy, industry operators will retain a large portion of customers gained during the recession by continuing to offer a diverse, comprehensive product range. Furthermore, as the economy recovers, average working hours are expected to increase, which will contribute to less leisure time for consumers. As a result, the one-stop-shop format of supercenters and warehouse clubs will help the industry take advantage of rising consumer demand for convenience. Therefore, stores will likely require more employees for daily operations, as store traffic continues to increase. To meet this demand, companies will hire more workers and so employment is expected to increase at an annualized 3.7%, from 1.6 million workers in 2014 to 1.9 million in 2019.

Global Industry:

A. **Industry Definition:** The hypermarkets and super centers sector is valued as the total revenues of the 30 leading companies engaged in superstore and hypermarket/super center retail. The performance of the market is forecast to decelerate, with an anticipated compound annual growth rate (CAGR) of 4.0% for the five-year period 2011 - 2016, which is expected to drive the market to a value of $2,197.5 billion by the end of 2016.

B. **Market Size and Growth Rate:** The global hypermarkets & super centers sector produced good but decelerating growth to moderate growth between 2008 and 2010. However the market returned to strong growth in 2011 and is expected to produce moderate growth through to the end of the forecast period in 2016. The global hypermarkets & super centers sector had total revenue of $1,809.0 billion in 2011, representing a compound annual growth rate (CAGR) of 6.0% between 2007 and 2011. In comparison the European and Asia-Pacific regions produced revenue $912.3 billion and $202.4 billion respectively in 2011. The performance of the market is forecast to decelerate, with an anticipated CAGR of 4.0% for the five-year period 2011 - 2016, which is expected to drive the market to a value of $2,197.5 billion by the end of 2016.

C. **Key Rivals & Market Share:** Walmart is the leading player in the global hypermarkets & super centers sector, accounting a 23.2% share of the sector's value. Carrefour SA accounts for a further 7% of the sector.

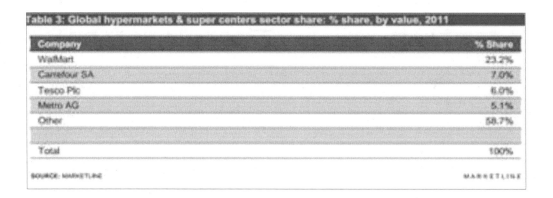

Table 3: Global hypermarkets & super centers sector share: % share, by value, 2011

Company	% Share
WalMart	23.2%
Carrefour SA	7.0%
Tesco Plc	6.0%
Metro AG	5.1%
Other	58.7%
Total	100%

SOURCE: MARKETLINE   MARKETLINE

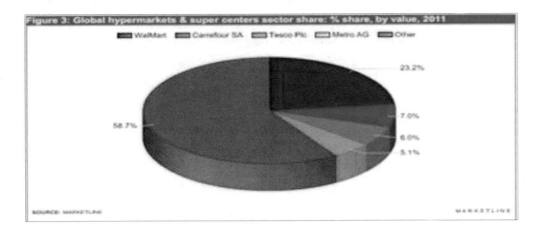

Figure 3: Global hypermarkets & super centers sector share: % share, by value, 2011

- WalMart
- Carrefour SA
- Tesco Plc
- Metro AG
- Other

23.2%

7.0%

6.0%

5.1%

58.7%

SOURCE: MARKETLINE   MARKETLINE

D. **Scope of Competitive Rivalry:** Despite the tendency towards consolidation within some individual countries markets, the global hypermarket and supercenter sector is remains relatively fragmented, with a large number of players operating. However, a clear leader is present in Wal-Mart, which accounts for around a quarter of global revenues. Other companies such as Carrefour and Tesco also possess significant shares. Global hypermarkets and super-centers continue to compete with a variety of local, national and international chains in the discount, department, drug, specialty and wholesale sectors of the retail sector. A number of players have successfully diversified their operations to include businesses such as consumer financial services (e.g. credit cards and insurance), reducing reliance on this sector alone. Moreover, a number of players have also diversified the way in which they distribute products. For example, Tesco and Wal-Mart now offer online retail services. Rivalry is intensified between players due to a number of factors including the absence of consumer switching costs. However, strong sector growth lessens competition. Rivalry is moderate in this sector overall.

E. **Concentration vs Fragmentation:** The global hypermarket and super-center sector is remains relatively fragmented, with a large number of players operating. However, a clear leader is present in Wal-Mart (which accounts for around a quarter of global revenues), which accounts for around a quarter of global revenues. Other companies such as Carrefour and Tesco also possess significant shares. Global hypermarkets and super-centers continue to compete with a variety of local, national and international chains in the discount, department, drug, specialty and wholesale sectors of the retail sector. The global hypermarkets and super centers sector is tending towards increased concentration, with a large number of players operating within international and local markets.

F. **Number of Buyers:** Sector players have a wide variety of potential customers, which weakens buyer power. Hypermarkets and super centers sell a diverse range of products such as food, clothing, health and beauty products, sporting goods, entertainment (CDs, DVDs, games), and more. Such diversity increases the customer base of companies, thereby reducing overall buyer power. Although consumers in this sector may be loyal to particular brands, when it comes to particular merchandise, price competition is often strong between the retailers themselves.

G. **Demand Determinants:** "A number of manufactures have formed strong brands, which returns in many market players stocking products to meet end-consumer demand. The increasing number of participants manufacturing own brands puts much strain on the suppliers.

H. **Degree of Product Differentiation:** "A threat of substitution to hypermarkets and super centers comes from the specialty store sector. Specialty stores offer a greater variety of products within a single category, as opposed to many different categories, perhaps catering for the higher-end as well as mass-consumer segments, and being able to offer greater customer guidance and support. However, hypermarkets and super centers offer the convenience of shopping for different products in one location. Another threat to food retail is foodservice. Such alternatives offer convenience for consumers; however they are a more costly option. Other alternatives include subsistence farming, which is still present in a number of major global economies. However, it is unlikely that such substitutes will become a complete alternative for food retail. Overall, the threat of substitutes is moderate.

I. **Product Innovation:** A number of manufacturers have established strong brands, which results in many market players stocking products to meet end consumer demand. However, the increasing number of players manufacturing own brand products, puts many suppliers under significant pressure.

J. **Key Success Factors:** A number of participants have triumphantly diversified their operations to include organizations such as consumer financial services (credit cards, insurance), reducing dependency on this sector alone.

K. **Supply/Demand Conditions:** There is a change from supply side to becoming more demand driven by the consumer. Retailers in emerging markets will continue to enjoy strong consumer demand.

L. **Analysis of Stage in Life Cycle:** This industry is in the mature stage of the life cycle.

M. **Pace of Technological Change:** This industry is in the mature stage of the life cycle.

N. **Vertical Integration:** Hypermarkets and supercenters have been involved in backwards vertical integration by coming up with private labels that are sold within their stores such as Walmart US and Costco.

O. **Economies of Scale:** New entrants will have difficulty competing with larger incumbents who benefit from scale economies in purchasing, distribution and advertising.

P. **Barriers to Entry:** Large hypermarkets and super centers, such as Wal-Mart, benefit from significant scale economies in purchasing, distribution and advertising. In order to set up a large hypermarket or super center, significant capital is required to purchase merchandise, buy or lease premises in which to sell the merchandise, and to hire and train employees. Advertising, in order to boost awareness of an unfamiliar retail brand, may also add to costs. In some countries, players may face difficulties in obtaining planning permission for large-scale retail outlets, and the legal and administrative costs of appealing against unfavorable planning decisions can add an additional entry barrier not encountered in other retail sectors. Small companies may be able to compete effectively by offering different brands or types of merchandise. Introducing technology such as self-service checkouts, which attract customers through increased convenience and reduce staff expenditure, can help new players to compete. Strong sector growth also appeals to new entrants. Overall, there is a moderate likelihood of new entrants to this sector.

Q. **Regulation/Deregulation:** Regulation is increasing in the global marketplace as health concerns are becoming problematic. Regulation may differ from region to region as well as local governing bodies.

R. **Globalization:** Global hypermarkets and super centers sector is made up of the following geographic segments:

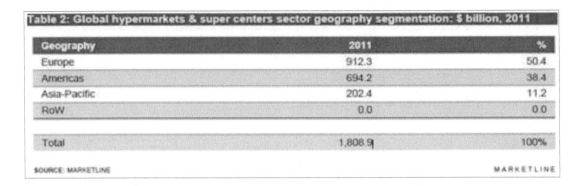

Geography	2011	%
Europe	912.3	50.4
Americas	694.2	38.4
Asia-Pacific	202.4	11.2
RoW	0.0	0.0
Total	1,808.9	100%

Table 2: Global hypermarkets & super centers sector geography segmentation: $ billion, 2011

SOURCE: MARKETLINE

MARKETLINE

S. **Trends:** The global hypermarkets and super centers sector is tending towards increased concentration, with a large number of players operating within international and local markets.

Porter's Five Forces Analysis

Buyer Power:

Players have a wide variety of potential customers, which weakens buyer power. Hypermarkets and super centers sell a diverse range of products such as food, clothing, health and beauty products, sporting goods, entertainment (CDs, DVDs, games), and more. Such diversity increases the customer base of companies, thereby reducing overall buyer power. Although consumers in this sector may be loyal to particular brands, when it comes to particular merchandise, price competition is often strong between the retailers themselves. Some retailers are responding to this by offering products that appeal across the socioeconomic spectrum. For instance, Tesco offers 'Value' and 'Finest' product ranges, each intended to appeal to a specific income group. Buyer power is strengthened to an extent by the fact that switching costs are generally low. However, a number of companies run reward programs for frequent shoppers. Buyer power is moderate.

Supplier Power:

Suppliers of products to the hypermarkets and super centers sector include manufacturers, distributors, farmers, agricultural cooperatives (grains, fruit and vegetables, meat and fish, dairy products etc.), and companies that provide packaging materials. Large retailers buy from a large number of suppliers, ensuring that they are not reliant on any particular supplier. Companies may have long-term relationships with suppliers; however there are generally few long-term contracts as they impose switching costs. Distributors buy products from manufacturers and resell them to retailers. Distributors often enter into contracts with retailers, with contracts being terminable after a notice period and this can incur switching costs for suppliers, decreasing their power. The general fall of import tariffs, particularly in the US, has allowed store retailers to source goods produced in areas of low-cost labor, whilst also providing companies with additional bargaining power when dealing with suppliers due to the influx of competition. However, a number of manufacturers have established strong brands, which results in many players stocking products to meet end-consumer demand. The increasing numbers of players offering own-brand products put many brand-name suppliers under significant pressure. Supplier power is assessed as moderate.

New Entrants:

Large hypermarkets and super centers, such as Wal-Mart, benefit from significant scale economies in purchasing, distribution and advertising. In order to set up a large hypermarket or super center, significant capital is required to purchase merchandise, buy or lease premises in which to sell the merchandise, and to hire and train employees. Advertising, in order to boost awareness of an unfamiliar retail brand, may also add to costs. In some countries, players may face difficulties in obtaining planning permission for large-scale retail outlets, and the legal and administrative costs of appealing against unfavorable planning decisions can add an additional entry barrier not encountered in other retail sectors. Small companies may be able to compete effectively by offering different brands or types of merchandise. Introducing technology such as self-service checkouts, which attract customers through increased convenience and reduce staff expenditure, can help new players to compete. Strong sector growth also appeals to new entrants. There is a moderate likelihood of new entrants to this industry.

Threat of Substitutes:

A threat of substitution to hypermarkets and super centers comes from the specialty store sector. Specialty stores offer a greater variety of products within a single category, as opposed to many different categories, perhaps catering for the higher-end as well as mass-consumer segments, and being able to offer greater customer guidance and support. However, hypermarkets and super centers offer the convenience of shopping for different products in one location. Another threat to food retail is foodservice. Such alternatives offer convenience for consumers; however they are a more costly option. Other alternatives include subsistence farming, which is still present in a number of major global economies. However, it is unlikely that such substitutes will become a complete alternative for food retail. The threat of substitutes is moderate.

Degree of Rivalry:

Despite the tendency towards consolidation within some individual countries markets, the global hypermarket and super center industry remains relatively fragmented, with a large number of players operating. Wal-Mart accounts for around a quarter of global revenues. Global hypermarkets and super-centers continue to compete with a variety of local, national and international chains in the discount, department, drug, specialty and wholesale sectors of the retail sector. A number of players have successfully diversified their operations to include businesses such as consumer financial services (e.g. credit cards and insurance), reducing reliance on this sector alone. Rivalry is intensified between players due to a number of factors including the absence of consumer switching costs. However, strong industry growth lessens competition. Rivalry is moderate in this industry.

Porter's Five Forces Analysis Summary

- The global hypermarkets and super centers sector is tending towards increased concentration, with a large number of players operating within international and local markets.
- Overall rivalry is assessed as moderate
- Weak buyer power due to the wide variety of potential customers and high competition amongst players
- A threat of substitution to hypermarkets and super centers comes from the specialty store sector.
- Players have started manufacturing their own brand products. Thus putting many suppliers under significant pressure to sale products at reasonable prices
- New entrants will have difficulty competing with larger, more established players who benefit from scale economies in purchasing, distribution and advertising
  - High capital requirements and planning permission for massive retail outlets will discourage new entrants

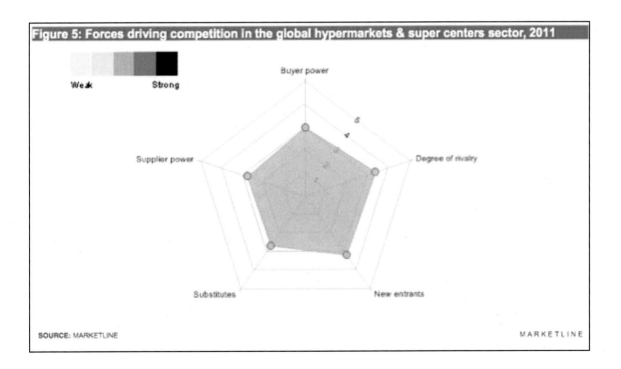

Figure 5: Forces driving competition in the global hypermarkets & super centers sector, 2011

SOURCE: MARKETLINE

MARKETLINE

<u>Organization Structure:</u>

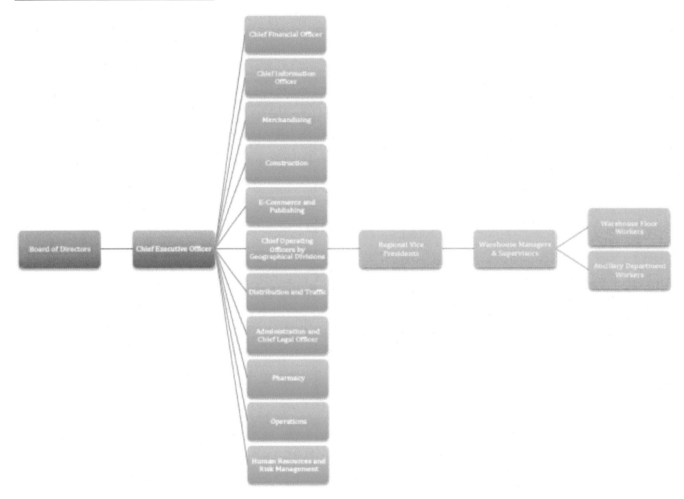

A. **Advantages and Disadvantages:**

A divisional organizational structure gives a company the ability to segregate large sections of the company's business into semi-autonomous groups. A divisional organizational structure consists of several parallel teams focusing on a division. Unlike departments, divisions are more autonomous, each with its own top executive--often a vice president--and typically manage their own hiring, budgeting and advertising.

Divisions work well because they allow a team to focus on their divisional area, with a leadership structure that supports its major strategic objectives. Having its own vice president makes it more likely the division will receive the resources it needs from the company. Also, a division's focus allows it to build a common culture that contributes both to higher morale and a better knowledge of the division's portfolio. Division "structures offer significant advantages over functional structures in terms of facilitating the management of a complex and diverse set of operations." (Thompson, 2012) Additional advantages include:

a. Places business-level strategy in the hands of divisional executives.

b. Leaves corporate-level strategy in the hands of top executives.

c. Minimizes costs of coordinating division wide activities

d. Enhances top executives ability to control a diverse and complex organization.

e. Align individual goals with that of the organization.

f. Increases productivity as it promotes competition among divisions.

A divisional structure also has disadvantages as well. A company comprised of competing divisions may allow office politics instead of sound strategic thinking to affect its view on such matters as allocation of company resources. Also, divisions can bring compartmentalization that can lead to incompatibilities. Some other disadvantages include:

a. Can inhibit cross-business collaboration.

b. Failure to capture cross-business synergies.

Financial Analysis:

Costco Financial Ratios:

Liquidity Ratio	Costco 2013	Costco 2012	Costco 2011
Current Ratio	1.2	1.1	1.14
Quick Ratio	0.6	0.53	0.52
Working capital	2.583	1.266	1.656
Activity Ratio	**Costco 2013**	**Costco 2012**	**Costco 2011**
Inventory Turnover	11.65	12.24	11.71
Total Asset Turnover	3.47	3.65	3.32
Days of Inventory	31.34	29.83	31.17
Profitability Ratios	**Costco 2013**	**Costco 2012**	**Costco 2011**
Gross Profit Margin	12.56	12.42	12.57
Operating Profit Margin	2.9	2.78	2.74
Net Profit Margin	1.94	1.72	1.64
Return on Total Assets	6.73	6.3	5.46
Return on Stockholders Equity	18.52	13.65	11.63
Price-Earnings Ratio	24.19	24.82	24.52
Leverage Ratio	**Costco 2013**	**Costco 2012**	**Costco 2011**
Debt to Total Asset Ratio	63.64	53.88	53.02
Debt to Equity Ratio	175	116.81	112.85
Long-Term Debt to Equity Ratio	54.61	18.87	17.01

Walmart Financial Ratios:

Liquidity Ratio	Walmart 2013	Walmart 2012	Walmart 2011
Current Ratio	0.84	0.88	0.89
Quick Ratio	0.23	0.23	0.27
Working capital	-11.878	-7.325	-6.591
Activity Ratio	**Walmart 2013**	**Walmart 2012**	**Walmart 2011**
Inventory Turnover	8.05	8.23	8.67
Total Asset Turnover	2.31	2.31	2.33
Days of Inventory	45.38	44.34	42.09
Profitability Ratios	**Walmart 2013**	**Walmart 2012**	**Walmart 2011**
Gross Profit Margin	24.87	25.02	25.34
Operating Profit Margin	5.49	5.46	5.58
Net Profit Margin	3.62	3.51	3.89
Return on Total Assets	8.37	8.11	9.07
Return on Stockholders Equity	20.8	20.72	23
Price-Earnings Ratio	14.57	13.61	12.52
Leverage Ratio	**Walmart 2013**	**Walmart 2012**	**Walmart 2011**
Debt to Total Asset Ratio	59.76	60.83	60.59
Debt to Equity Ratio	148.48	155.28	153.74
Long-Term Debt to Equity Ratio	60.62	73.05	71.49

Carrefour Financial Ratios:

Liquidity Ratio	Carrefour 2013	Carrefour 2012	Carrefour 2011
Current Ratio	0.84	0.9	0.74
Quick Ratio	0.53	0.59	0.46
Working capital	-3.368	-2.163	-6.852
Activity Ratio	**Carrefour 2013**	**Carrefour 2012**	**Carrefour 2011**
Inventory Turnover	10.48	9.83	9.38
Total Asset Turnover	1.8	1.74	1.72
Days of Inventory	35.06	33.59	38.51
Profitability Ratios	**Carrefour 2013**	**Carrefour 2012**	**Carrefour 2011**
Gross Profit Margin	20.17	19.71	18.04
Operating Profit Margin	2.94	2.75	-0.14
Net Profit Margin	1.64	1.57	0.46
Return on Total Assets	3.54	3.02	1.99
Return on Stockholders Equity	16.71	17.48	4.58
Price-Earnings Ratio	15.83	10.69	32.02
Leverage Ratio	**Carrefour 2013**	**Carrefour 2012**	**Carrefour 2011**
Debt to Total Asset Ratio	21.66	24.94	23.69
Debt to Equity Ratio	117.72	150.21	168.93
Long-Term Debt to Equity Rati	96.26	119.98	136.31

Liquidity Ratios:

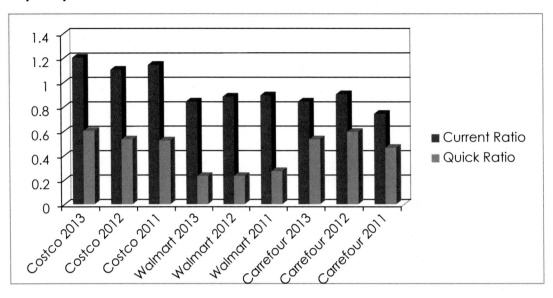

Costco is positioned the best compared to their competition to pay liabilities using assets that can be converted to cash.

Working Capital:

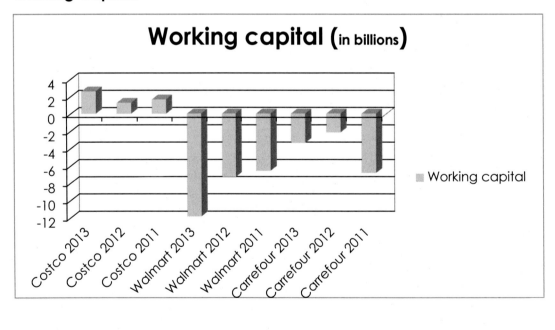

Costco is the leader in terms of being able pay their current liabilities in a timely basis and they are also in the best position to not have to resort to borrowing or raising more equity capital.

Activity Ratio:

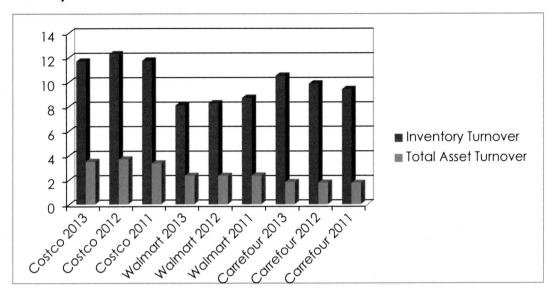

Costco has the highest number of inventory turns per year compared to their competition.

Days of Inventory:

Costco's has the fewest days of inventory management comparative to their competitors. So they are extremely efficient in this measurement.

Profitability Margins:

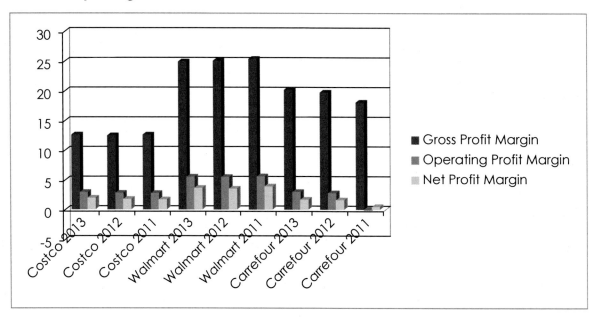

Costco's Gross Profit margin, Operating Profit margin and Net Profit Margin have been extremely consistent over the past 3 years. Their trend has been going upward.

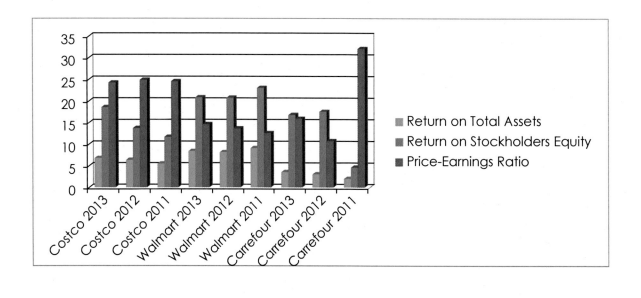

The trend for Costco's return on investments has increased each year. The Costco Return on Stockholders Equity has earned investors between 12% and 18%. They have also increased each year. The Costco Price-Earnings ratio show that investors all have high confidence in firm's outlook and growth.

Altman Z Score:

Altman Z Score	2013	2012	2011
Costco	5.72	6.18	5.46
Walmart	4.29	4.25	4.31
Carrefour	2.09	1.83	1.51

In comparison of the Altman Z Score, which determines the likelihood that a company may face bankruptcy, Costco is in strong financial shape. Any score below 1.8 signifies the company may be headed towards bankruptcy and a score above 3.0 signifies strong financial health. Carrefour scored very low in both 2011 and 2012, however, found a little stability in 2013. Costco scored better than Walmart and Carrefour in the three consecutive years.

Tobin's Q:

Tobins Q	2013	2012	2011
Costco	1.69	1.56	1.26
Walmart	1.54	1.56	1.22
Carrefour	0.33	0.30	0.26

Costco and Walmart scored high in the Tobins Q, however Carrefour scored poorly. Tobins Q represents the market value compared to the recorded assets of the company. A score above 1 signifies the company's market value is greater than their recorded assets. Costco increased their score from 1.26 in 2011 to 1.693 in 2013.

Dupont Analysis:

The DuPont Analysis reflects the three areas that effect Return on Equity: operating efficiency, asset usage efficiency, and financial leverage. This breakdown can help identify which area of the business that is underperforming.

Costco

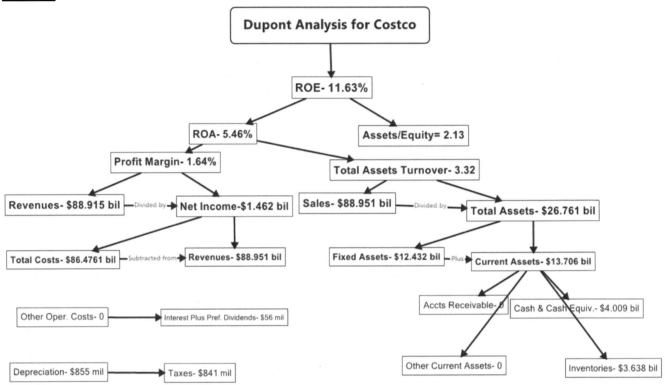

Costco's ROE in 2011 was 11.63%, with ROA of 5.46% and Assets/Equity of 2.13

Walmart

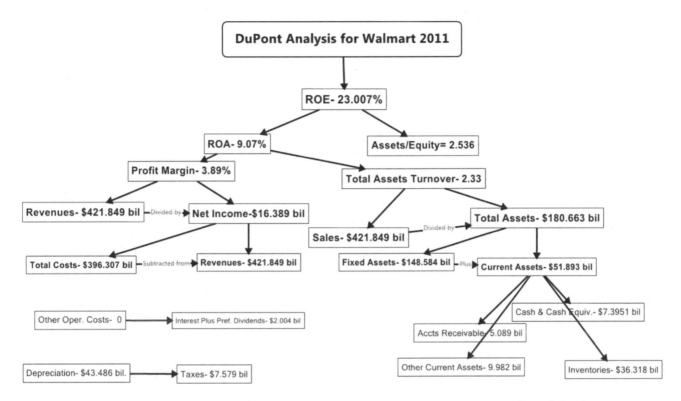

Walmart's ROE in 2011 was 23%, with ROA of 9.07% and Assets/Equity of 2.536

Carrefour

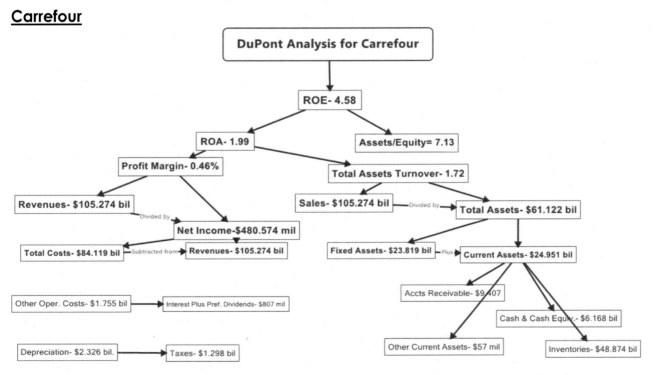

Carrefour's ROE in 2011 was 4.58%, with ROA of 1.99% and Assets/Equity of 7.13

SWOT Analysis:

Costco operates an international chain of membership warehouses. The company offers an attractive value proposition to its customers, which enables it to drive customer traffic and generate strong membership renewals. However, the increasing labor costs and healthcare costs in its key market may affect the company's profitability.

Strengths	Weaknesses
Price positioning leads to increased customer loyalty Low cost operating model Sustainability initiatives Strong financial position	Limited product choice Overdependence on the US and Canadian markets
Opportunities	Threats
Growing online retail sales Growing demand for private label brands Resurgence in the US housing market	Increasing labor and healthcare costs Foreign exchange rate fluctuations High exposure to low growth mature markets

Strengths

Price positioning leads to increased customer loyalty:

Costco positioned itself as a price leader to acquire market share. Costco maintains a maximum markup of 15% for branded and private label products. Private label items offer at least 20% savings compared to the leading national brand. The average markup on the company's merchandise is much lower compared to more than 25% at supermarkets and department stores. Furthermore, over the online retail channel, the company's markup is even lower. Offering attractive value proposition to the customers acts as a competitive advantage for the company. Value price positioning enables Costco to drive customer traffic and generate strong membership renewals. The company's membership renewal rate was 90% in the US and Canada, and 86% worldwide in FY2013. The penetration of executive membership offered by Costco apart from its other membership programs has also been increasing. Though the fees charged for executive membership is the highest compared with other Costco's membership programs, the popularity of the executive membership is growing because of further value offered to the members through the 2% reward program. This program offers an additional 2% (up to a maximum of approximately $750 per year) discount to the members on qualified purchases that can be redeemed at Costco warehouses. To drive the increase in executive member signups, Costco increased the rewards cap from $500 to $750 in 2011. The executive member base constituted 38% of the primary memberships in FY2013. Although they represent a little over one-third of Costco's overall customers, they account for more than two-third of its revenues. At the end of second quarter of FY2014 (three months ending February 16, 2014), the company's paid executive members were more than 14 million, an increase of 200,000 over the last 12 weeks.

In the recent past, there has been an increase in the price sensitive customer base and industry reports suggest the increase in demand for value products at low price points. In the economy characterized by cautious consumer spending, value retailers and warehouse retailers are expected to fare well. Thus, shift in consumer preference for value products and the attractive price proposition of Costco will enable the company to attract a large customer base. Additionally, the customer loyalty the company enjoys will enable it to retain customers in a highly competitive market.

Low cost operating model:

Costco's processes are made efficient at every point, which, in turn, helps the company to maintain margins despite low price positioning. The company offers only a limited selection of national brands and private labels across a wide merchandise range. Since these are offered at low prices, the inventory turnover is very rapid which reduces the inventory costs. Costco encourages volume purchasing and therefore, the sales volume is kept high despite low prices. The company's high sales volume and rapid inventory turnover enable it to sell and be paid for inventory before Costco is required to pay the merchandise vendors. As and when the sales increase and inventory turnover becomes more rapid, a greater percentage of inventories are financed through payment terms provided by suppliers rather than by the working capital, thereby reducing the company's financing costs.

Additionally, the company's streamlined distribution network also enables it to reduce certain redundant costs. Costco's depots receive container-based shipments from manufacturers and reallocate these goods for shipment to the individual warehouses, generally in less than 24 hours. Through such a process, Costco maximizes freight volume and handling efficiencies which leads to low receiving costs as the process eliminates many of the costs associated with multiple-step distribution channels.

Costco relies on the attractive value proposition to gain customers and therefore operates no-frills, self-service warehouse facilities. Merchandise is stored on racks above the sales floor itself and pallets containing large quantities of each item are displayed, thereby reducing labor required for handling and stocking. The company engages in very limited marketing programs and only involves in direct marketing for promoting select merchandise. These efficient processes enable Costco to maintain its price positioning and sustain competition in the industry.

Sustainability initiatives:

To maintain its business in a sustainable and environmentally responsible manner, the company follows a four-fold approach. It focuses on reducing its carbon footprint, enhancing warehouse energy management systems, expanding packaging design initiatives, and developing its recycling and waste stream management systems. To reduce greenhouse gas emissions (GHG) it stopped using hydrochlorofluorocarbon (HCFC) refrigerant, an ozone-depleting substance, in new and replacement refrigeration systems in 2007 and discontinued its use in new and replacement air conditioning systems in 2008. The company also completed a GHG inventory for its operations in the US, Puerto Rico, Canada, the UK and Australia, which meets standards established by the GHG Protocol Corporate Accounting and Reporting Standard. Furthermore, Costco operates large rooftop solar photovoltaic systems at 78 of its facilities in Hawaii, California, New Mexico, New Jersey, Puerto Rico, Colorado and Arizona. These systems are projected to generate 69 million kilowatt-hours of electricity annually.

The company also recycles and renews waste generated by warehouses into usable products, biofuels or compost, or to use as feed stock. For instance, Costco recycled 210,000 tons of corrugated containers during FY2013, an increase of 23.5% since FY2010. In addition, the company's organic recycling programs diverted over 2,505 tons of food waste from landfills during FY2013; and its new electronic waste (E-waste) diversion program recycled 2,074 tons during the same period. Costco also focuses on eliminating polyvinyl chloride (PVC) plastic in its packaging and replacing it with recycled or recyclable materials. Therefore, through its focus on being environment friendly and its sustainability-driven innovation, the company can increase its product awareness, besides considerably reducing its costs and catering to the growing demand of green products.

Strong financial position:

Costco has witnessed a steady growth in its net sales over many years. The company's net sales increased at a compound annual growth rate (CAGR) of 10% from $69,889 million in FY2009 to $102,870 million in FY2013. As compared to FY2012, the net sales of Costco grew by 6% in FY2013. The growth in net sales is driven by a 6% increase in comparable sales and sales at warehouses opened during FY2012 and FY2013. Costco's profitability also increased significantly. The operating profit and net profit of the company grew at a CAGR of 14% and 17%, respectively, during FY2009–13. The operating profit and net profit grew by 10.7% and 19.3%, respectively, in FY2013 over FY2012. In addition to the income of the company, the other financial parameters have been impressive. Total cash and cash equivalents with Costco increased 31.6% from $3,528 million in FY2012 to $4,644 million in FY2013. Thus, strong financial performance will provide the company with financial flexibility and also help in expansion activities.

Weaknesses

Limited product choice:

Costco offers a limited selection of products. A typical Costco warehouse stocks an average of about 3,700 products for sale at a particular time. Many competitors of the company such as discount retailers, supermarkets and supercenters offer a larger selection of products at a particular time. For instance, The Home Depot offers approximately 40,000 products at its stores. Wal-Mart, another key competitor of the company, offers a vast selection of products. Customers prefer a seamless shopping experience and prefer one stop shop options. Thus, limited product offering may act as a competitive disadvantage and adversely impact the average spend of customers at Costco's stores.

Overdependence on the US and Canadian markets:

Costco is highly dependent on the US and Canada for revenue generation. In FY2013, the US and Canadian markets contributed 88.1% to the total sales of the company. Furthermore, within the US, the company is highly dependent on its California operations, which represented 23% of net sales in FY2013. The company also has a larger percentage of higher volume warehouses in California, compared to other markets. Any decline in the sales of the US and Canadian operations, particularly in California, due to weakening demand trends, increase in unemployment rates, increase in labor costs and other factors could significantly affect the company's sales.

Opportunities

Growing online retail sales:

Interactive online shopping is increasingly being preferred over traditional shopping by consumers who have become more vigilant about spending money. According to the US Department of Commerce, online retail sales (adjusted for seasonal variation) in the US increased from $165.8 billion in 2010 to $262.5 billion in 2013, representing a CAGR of 16.6%. E-commerce sales increased 17% in 2013 over the previous year. Total retail sales, on the other hand, grew by only 4.3% during 2013. E-commerce sales accounted for 5.8% of total retail sales in 2013, compared to 4.3% in 2010. A similar trend is noticed in Canada and the UK. According to Statistics Canada, more than half of the internet users ordered products and services online in 2012. The Canadian e-commerce sales are expected to grow at a rate of 10% during 2013–18 according to industry sources. The online retail sales in the UK are growing significantly in the past few years. According to the Office for National Statistics, non-seasonally adjusted average weekly value for internet retail sales in the UK was £554.2 million (approximately $866.9 million) in February 2013; this increased to £622.3 million (approximately $973.5 million) in February 2014, representing an increase of 12.3%. Internet sales accounted for 10% of the total retail sales (excluding automotive fuel) in February 2013. This figure increased to 10.7% in February 2014.

Costco operates its online business through its websites, www.costco.com, www.costco.ca and www.costco.co.uk. In FY2013, online sales accounted for nearly 3% of the company's consolidated net sales. Furthermore, the company introduced mobile applications for Apple and Android devices in 2012. Also, in 2013, the company's website was re-platformed to improve its user experience as well as increase growth capability. Therefore, Costco can leverage its online presence to serve a large customer base, which, in turn, will augment its revenue.

Growing demand for private label brands:

The private label market is growing at a fast pace in the US. According to industry sources, among all major US retail channels, private label sales increased by approximately 3% to reach nearly $109 billion in 2012. Since 2009, annual growth of store brands sales has averaged approximately 5%, compared to national brands sales annual growth of approximately 2%. Private label products provide customers with an attractive alternative to higher-priced national brands. Instead of buying expensive brands, consumers across the industry are turning to generic and private label products. Even upper-income shoppers are more willing to buy generic, which has traditionally appealed more to shoppers with limited budgets.

The company offers private label products under the Kirkland Signature brand. According to industry sources, private label products account for 20% of the company's total revenues. Costco has been growing its overall private label range over the years. With its strong brand image, Costco can leverage on the growth trend to increase sales from this category.

Resurgence in the US housing market:

The US housing market, which has experienced the lowest level of sales in the past several years, is showing signs of recovery. According to the US Census Bureau of the Department of Commerce, the construction spending in the US was at a seasonally adjusted annual rate of $942.5 billion in March 2014, an increase of 8.4% over the same period last year. In March 2014, residential construction contributed $374.5 billion to the total value. The residential construction spending grew by 15.2% in March 2014 compared to March 2013. In comparison, nonresidential construction contributed $568 billion to the total value in March 2014, an increase of 4.4% compared to March 2013. The company offers a wide range of home improvement products, including bathroom hardware, lighting products, flooring products, kitchen appliances, and other home improvement products such as alarms and detectors, doors and door hardware, fencing, gates and gate openers, furnace filters, and rain gutters. Therefore, improving construction market will enable the company to further expand its revenues and market share.

Threats

Increasing labor and healthcare costs:

There has been an increase in labor costs in the US in the recent years. The federal minimum wage rate in the US, which remained at $5.15 per hour since 1998, increased to $5.85 per hour in 2008. It further increased to $6.55 per hour in 2009 and to $7.25 per hour in 2010. Moreover, many states and municipalities in the country have minimum wage rate even higher than $7.25 per hour due to higher cost of living. The minimum wage rate has increased in the states of Arizona (from $7.8 in 2013 to $7.9 in 2014), Colorado (from $7.78 in 2013 to $8 in 2014), Missouri ($7.35 in 2013 to $7.5 in 2014), Ohio (from $7.85 in 2013 to $7.95 in 2014), Florida (from $7.79 in 2013 to $7.93 in 2014), Oregon (from $8.95 in 2013 to $9.1 in 2014), Rhode Island (from $7.75 in 2013 to $8 in 2014) and Washington (from $9.19 in 2013 to $9.32 in 2014) in the recent past. In addition, the increase in healthcare costs will also increase the company's operating costs. The Patient Protection and Affordable Care Act and the Health Care and Education Reconciliation Act were reenacted in the year 2010. These Acts expand the healthcare coverage to many uninsured individuals and also expand coverage to those already insured. According to industry estimates, healthcare costs for the US employers are estimated to grow by 7% in 2014 compared to 2013. Thus, increasing labor costs coupled with high healthcare expenses could increase the company's overall costs and affect its margins.

Foreign exchange rate fluctuations:

Though Costco's widespread geographic presence has its benefits, it also exposes the company to foreign exchange rate fluctuations. Costco has operations in the US, Puerto Rico, Canada, the UK, Korea, Taiwan, Japan, Mexico and Australia. Thus, the company generates revenue in many other currencies besides its domestic currency which is the US dollar. In FY2013, countries other than the US accounted for 28.2% of the company's overall revenue. Therefore, the company's revenues are subject to fluctuations in foreign exchange rates of all applicable currencies. While a strong US dollar decreases the revenues of the company, the weakening currency would have the reverse effect. During FY2013, changes in foreign currencies relative to the US dollar negatively impacted net sales by approximately $208, primarily due to the Japanese yen. Therefore, the revenues of the company are exposed to high risk due to the fluctuations in all applicable foreign exchange rates.

High exposure to low growth mature markets:

Retail markets in the developed economies like the US and the UK, where the company has presence, have been witnessing low consumer spending. Though the household spending in the UK has increased since 2009, the volume of goods and services purchased has experienced far lower growth. This indicates that the price increases have been greater than the increases in volume. High unemployment rate is one of the reasons for customers keeping their spending at low levels. According to the Office of National Statistics, unemployment rate in the UK was 6.9% for December 2013 to February 2014. Though this rate improved from an average of 8% in 2012, still remains high compared to other international markets. High unemployment rate is expected to further pressurize the economy of the UK.

In addition, the US market is also suffering from sluggish consumer spending and high unemployment rate. Though the consumer spending has increased in the US, it is growing at a very slow pace. The unemployment rate in the US was 6.3% in April 2014 according to the US Bureau of Labor Statistics. Though the rate of unemployment decreased from an average of 8.1% in 2012, it is still quite high compared with pre-recession times.

The US and the UK being the key markets for Costco, sluggish consumer spending and high unemployment rate in these markets can affect the sales growth, especially with respect to the sales of discretionary items such as computers and other big ticket electronic items.

TOWS Matrix:

	EXTERNAL OPPORTUNITIES(O)	EXTERNAL THREATS (T)
	1. Growing middle class amongst international markets 2. International market for warehouses and supercenters is growing rapidly 3. Annual growth of store brands sales has averaged approximately 5% compared to competitors 4. Increase in societal dependence on technology	1. Walmart, Target and Carrefour SA have larger employee population 2. Costco's revenues are subject to fluctuations in foreign exchange rates of all applicable currencies 3. Walmart/Target offer walk-in clinic services to anyone 4. BJ's Warehouse Club offers organic products
INTERNAL STRENGTHS (S)	**STRENGTHS OPPORTUNITIES (SO)**	**STRENGTHS THREATS (ST)**
1. Costco maintains a maximum markup of 15% for branded and private label products. 2. Average renewal rate of 90% in the US and Canada, and 86% worldwide. 3. Ability to maintain margins despite low price positioning 4. Steady growth in its net sales over many years.	1. Create international Kirkland Signature brand lines for international warehouses 2. Create Costco mobile application for members and potential to locate stores, view sales, access membership information	1. Create Costco walk-in clinics for members 2. Create Kirkland Signature Organic product line
INTERNAL WEAKNESSES (W)	**WEAKNESSES OPPORTUNITIES (WO)**	**WEAKNESSES THREATS (WT)**
1. Limited selection of products 2. Inabilty to obtain new executive talent due to low turnover 3. Overdependence on the US and Canadian markets	1. Increase social media presence on Facebook, Twitter, Instagram, Tumblr, etc 2. Open warehouses in countries with growing middle class (India, South Korea, Japan, etc) to alleviate strong Us and Canadian market dependence.	1. Solicit senior level management talent from competing companies to help company growth 2. Increase product line offerings to better compete in warehouse industry

External Opportunities (O):

a. Growing middle class amongst international markets.

b. International market for warehouses and supercenters is growing rapidly.

c. Annual growth of store brands sales has averaged approximately 5% compared to competitors.

d. Increase in societal dependence on technology.

External Threats (T):

a. Walmart, Target and Carrefour SA have larger employee population.

b. Costco's revenues are subject to fluctuations in foreign exchange rates of all applicable currencies.

c. Walmart/Target offer walk-in clinic services to anyone.

d. BJ's Warehouse Club offers organic products.

Internal Strengths (S):

a. Costco maintains a maximum markup of 15% for branded and private label products.

b. Average renewal rate of 90% in the US and Canada, and 86% worldwide.

c. Ability to maintain margins despite low price positioning.

d. Steady growth in its net sales over many years.

Strengths Opportunities (SO):

a. Create international Kirkland Signature brand lines for international warehouses.

b. Create Costco mobile application for members and potential to locate stores, view sales, access membership information.

Strengths Threats (ST):

a. Create Costco walk-in clinics for members.

b. Create Kirkland Signature Organic product line.

Internal Weakness (W):

a. Limited Selection of Products.

b. Inability to obtain new executive talent due to low turnover.

c. Overdependence on the US and Canadian Markets.

Weaknesses Opportunities (WO):

a. Increase social media presence on Facebook, Twitter, Instagram, Tumblr, etc.

b. Open warehouses in countries with growing middle class (India, South Korea, Japan, etc.) to alleviate strong US and Canadian market dependence.

Weaknesses Threats (WT):

a. Solicit senior level management from competition companies to help company growth.

b. Increase product line offering to better compete in warehouse industry.

Market Share Data Graphs:

Warehouse Clubs & Supercenters Domestic Market Share	
Costco Wholesale Corporation	17.1%
Walmart Stores Inc.	64.4%
Meijer Inc.	3.2%
BJ's Wholesale Club Inc.	2.6%
Target Corporation	2.2%
Other	10.5%

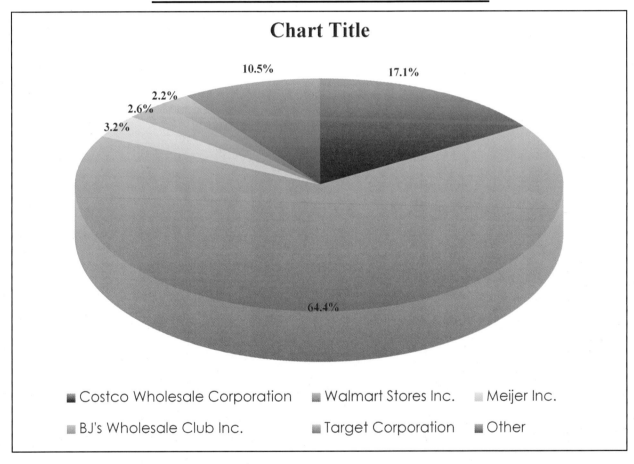

Warehouse Clubs & Supercenters Global Market Share	
Walmart Stores Inc.	23.2%
Carrefour SA	7.0%
Tesco Plc	6.0%
Metro AG	5.1%
Costco Wholesale Corpora	4.9%
Other	53.8%

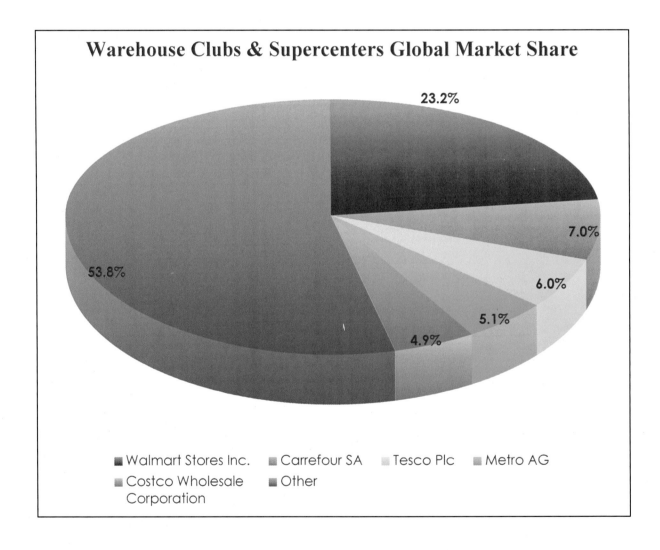

54

Focal Points for Actions:

Short Term:

General economic factors, domestically and internationally, may adversely affect our business, financial condition and results of operations.

- Examples: higher energy costs, inflation, levels of employment, healthcare costs, consumer debt levels, foreign exchange currency rate. These factors must be taken into consideration due to fluctuations coming up around domestic and international supply and demand, labor costs competition and market speculation. It can also increase our overall merchandise costs, and or selling, general and administrative costs.

We may not timely identify or effectively respond to consumer trends, which could negatively affect our relationship with our members, the demand for our products and services, and our market share.

- It is hard for us to predict what our members will demand year in and year out. We work to identify trends centered in on demographics and other consumer preferences. If we don't deliver it will have a negative effect on our rapport with our members, appeal for products and services and overall market share.

Vendors may be unable to supply us with quality merchandise at the right prices in a timely manner or may fail to adhere to our high standards resulting in adverse effects on our business, merchandise inventories, sales and profit margins.

- We deeply bank on the ability to purchase merchandise in ample quantities at aggressive prices. These terms on these supplies, prices or access to new products can change at any time. We purchase from both domestic and international manufactures and they have to adhere to quality standards and other factors. And finally our many suppliers are subject to many risks including labor disputes, union organizing activities and supply constraints.

Disruptions in our depot operations could adversely affect sales and member satisfaction.

- Costco places great emphasis on maintaining efficient depot operations such as receiving and distribution of merchandise. Such events that may cause a disruption in depot operations should carry negative consequences such as operational inefficiencies. This in turn could cause a decrease in sales and dissatisfaction amongst members.

We are involved in a number of legal proceedings and audits and, while we cannot predict the outcomes of such proceedings and other contingencies with certainty, some of these outcomes could adversely affect our business, financial condition and results of operations.

- The defense of lawsuits may involve significant expense and may divert management's attention and resources. The results of these events could negatively impact Costco's financial results as well as their operations.

If we do not maintain the privacy and security of member-related and business information, we could damage our reputation with members, incur substantial additional costs and become subject to litigation.

- Costco receives, retains, and transmits certain personal information about their members as well as credit card and other cashless payment methods. A beach in security could negatively impact the financial health of the company, tarnish their reputation and face legal action from those affected. This in turn would require Costco to spend a significant amount of capital to upgrade information security as well as temporarily disrupt Costco's online sales.

Long Term:

We face strong competition from other retailers and warehouse club operators, which could adversely affect our business, financial condition and results of operations.

- Costco faces competitive pressure due to the nature of the industry. Some of Costco's competitors may have greater financial resources, better market penetration, and better access to merchandise. Costco's inability to respond to the competitive pressures, changes in member's expectations and changes in retail markets may result in a loss of market share and a negative impact in financials.

We are highly dependent on the financial performance of our U.S. and Canadian operations.

- Costco's financial and operational performance is heavily dependent on the US and Canadian markets, which comprises more than 80% of consolidated net sales and operating income. Any substantial decline or slowing of these markets can adversely affect their business and financial performance. Declines in financial performance will inhibit Costco's growth throughout these markets as well as across the globe.

We may be unsuccessful implementing our growth strategy, including expanding our business, both in existing markets and in new markets, which could have an adverse impact on our business, financial condition and results of operations.

- Costco's future growth is partly dependent on the ability to acquire property, and find sustainable locations to build or lease new warehouses. Some local jurisdictions may incorporate laws that prohibit or slow the expansion in new and existing areas whereby forcing Costco to alter their course of action. Further, Costco will expand into existing markets where Costco warehouses exist. Local residents and businesses visit the warehouses from the local area. Costco may build in these areas that may cannibalize other Costco warehouses and directly impact their sales. Costco will expand into new markets that may create challenges such as difficulties in attracting customers due to the lack of brand awareness, as well as Costco's lack of awareness for member's preferences, and seasonal differences in the market.

Our failure to maintain positive membership loyalty and brand recognition could adversely affect our results of operations.

- Membership loyalty is essential to Costco's business model. Damage to the brand or reputation may negatively impact warehouse sales, lower employee morale and productivity, diminish member trust and thereby reducing member renewal rates. If members do not renew, this will adversely affect the financial performance of Costco and shareholder value. Also, Kirkland brand is Costco's private label brand. Sales of the Kirkland brand attract higher margins which increase the financial performance of the company. Any damage to the Kirkland brand or reputation may result in lower sales of Kirkland products, thereby reducing profitability and shareholder value.

Our international operations subject us to risks associated with the legislative, judicial, accounting, regulatory, political and economic factors specific to the countries or regions in which we operate which could adversely affect our business, financial condition and results of operations.

- Costco plans to accelerate the growth in international markets. As a result, it is conceivable that international operations will make up a larger portion of sales compared with the amount of sales it draws today. Future operating results could be adversely impacted due to circumstances that are out of the company's control. These factors include political conditions, economic conditions, regulatory constraints, currency regulations and foreign exchange rates, foreign trade, monetary and fiscal policies, and the laws and regulations of foreign governments. Many warehouse are located or will be located in countries that are less stable than the US. This could result in negative consequences inherent in international operations such as extended costs and difficulties of managing international operations, tax consequences, and difficulties in enforcing intellectual property rights.

If we do not successfully develop and maintain a relevant multichannel experience for our members, our results of operations could be adversely impacted.

- Multichannel retailing is rapidly evolving and Costco must keep pace with changing member expectations and new developments by competitors. There is a drastic increasing in using computers, tablets and mobile devices to shop online. To be successful Costco is investing in new technology and web platforms. If Costco cannot keep pace with the changes in technology and adapt in a timely manner, the company may experience a loss of consumer confidence, lost sales, and data security breaches which could adversely affect operational performance and brand reputation.

Develop Alternatives:

Industry Life Cycle:

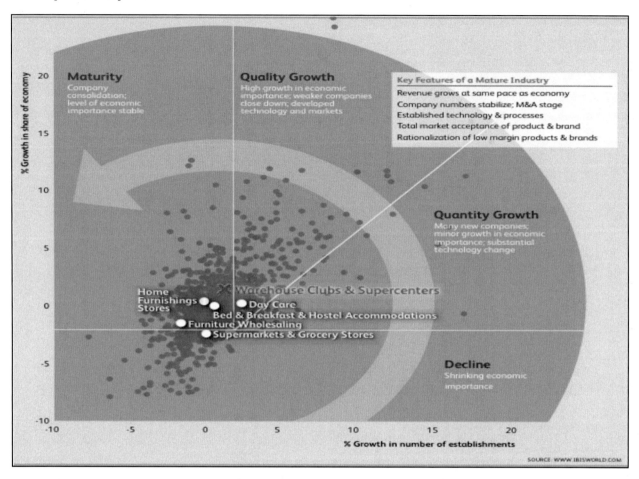

The domestic Warehouse Clubs and Supercenters industry is in the mature phase of its life cycle. In the 10 years to 2019, industry value added, a measure of the industry's contribution to the US economy, is forecast to increase at a rate of 3.9% per year on average. Comparatively, GDP is projected to rise at an annualized 2.7% over the same period. A slowdown in revenue growth and the moderation of profit; however, are expected to steady the industry's contribution to GDP. In addition, the number of industry enterprises has declined due to mergers and acquisitions during the five years to 2014, indicating the industry's mature state.

The global hypermarkets and Supercenter industry is in the mature stage of its life cycle as well. The compound annual growth rate of this industry between 2011 and 2016 is 4%. This period will exhibit a deceleration of growth compared with a CAGR of

6% for the period of 2007 to 2011. The industry in general has seen a slowdown of innovation and has focused on other value drivers such as price and private label brand development.

Boston Consulting Group Matrix:

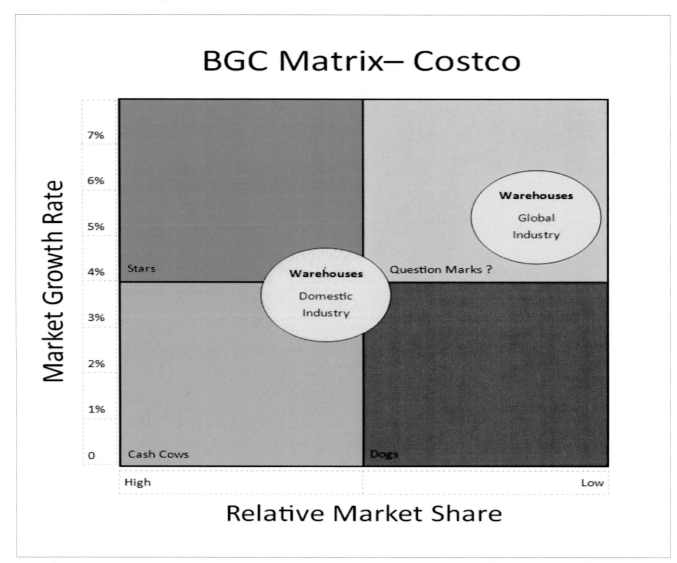

The market growth rate has slowed in the recent years for the domestic industry, however Costco commands a much larger share than it does in the global industry. Costco is a challenger to Walmart in the domestic industry and falls more into the category of "Cash Cow". However, looking at the global industry, Costco market share is much smaller in comparison to its rivals and the industry in general. The global industry growth rate is higher than that of the domestic industry growth rate. In the case of the global industry, Costco falls into the category of "Question Marks".

Competitive Position:

<u>Domestic</u>

Costco is a strong challenger to the industry leader, Walmart, in the domestic Warehouse and Supercenter industry. In fact, if Sam's Club, which is the warehouse entity owned by Walmart, were accounted for separately, Costco would emerge as the clear leader. However, if we look at Walmart inclusive of Sam's Club, Walmart leads the industry. Costco's revenue for their fiscal year end was $87.048 billion while Walmart's revenue for their fiscal year end 2011 was $421.85 billion. Included in Walmart's figure is Sam's Club revenue which was $45.459 billion.

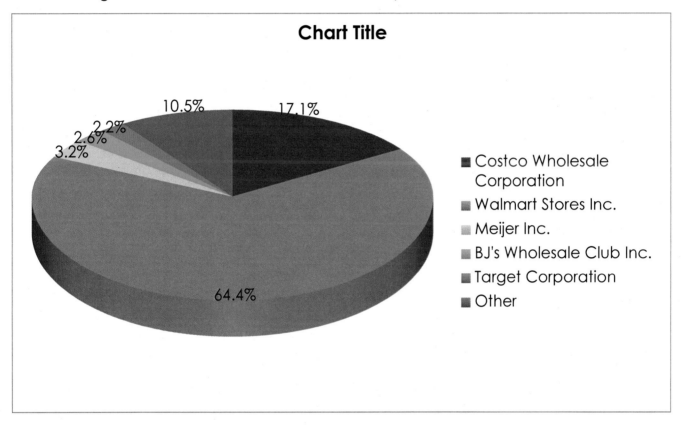

Chart Title

- Costco Wholesale Corporation
- Walmart Stores Inc.
- Meijer Inc.
- BJ's Wholesale Club Inc.
- Target Corporation
- Other

17.1%
10.5%
2.2%
2.6%
3.2%
64.4%

Global

Costco is a follower in the Global Hypermarkets and Supercenters industry. Walmart is the undisputed leader in the industry with Carrefour as the distant challenger, followed by Tesco's a follower along with Costco. The industry, attributed with $1.809 trillion in combined revenue in 2011, is expected to grow $2.197 trillion by the end of 2016. Again, Walmart made up a large portion of with $421.85 billion, followed by Carrefour with $105.274 billion, Tesco at $100.053 billion and Costco with 87.048 billion.

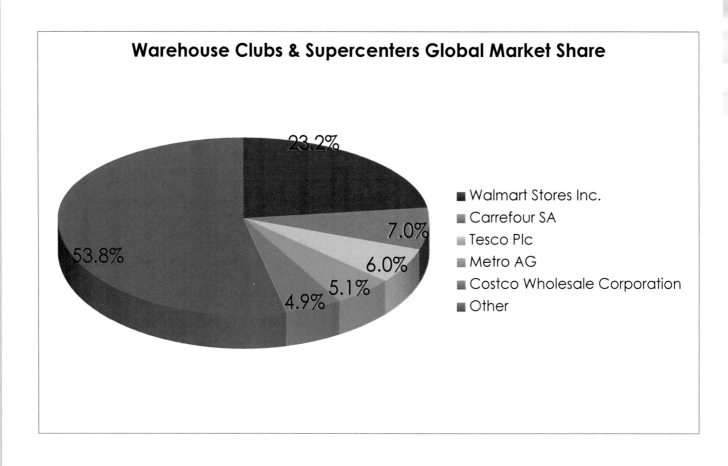

Competitive Strategy Options:

Costco can easily fit into the category of low cost leader. Costco's mission is to "provide our members with quality goods and services, at the lowest possible prices". The company's management and employees embrace this mission and continually work to ensure they execute upon it. While this strategy may seem to fit Costco and their mission, their competitive strategy is focused on being the Best Cost Provider.

"Best-cost provider strategies combine a strategic emphasis on low cost with a strategic emphasis on more than minimal quality, service, features, or performance. The aim is to create a competitive advantage by giving buyers more value for the money—an approach that entails matching close rivals on key quality/service/features/performance attributes and beating them on the costs of incorporating such attributes into the product or service." (Thompson, 2014) Companies using this strategy produce products or services of rather reputable quality that they sell at a competitive price. This particular strategy incorporates a mix of product differentiation and lower cost production and works best when customers are price sensitive and where buyer diversity makes product differentiation the norm.

Costco embodies the Best Cost Provider competitive strategy. This is evident when we look at Costco's total inventory turnover in comparison to that of Walmart and Carrefour. In 2011, Costco's inventory turnover ratio was 11.71 compared with Walmart's of 8.67, and Carrefour of 9.38. Costco has demonstrated the ability to turn their product over faster than their key rivals.

Rumelt's Criteria:

Rumelt's Criteria	Consistency	Consolance	Feasability	Advantage	Total
Market Penetration	5	5	4	5	19
Market Development	4	5	5	5	19
Product Development	4	4	5	5	18
Strategic Alliance	5	5	5	5	18
Horizontal Integration	5	4	4	5	18
Retrenchment	2	3	3	3	10
Conglomerate Diversification	3	3	2	3	11
Backwards Vertical Integration	2	2	2	3	9

The Rumelt's Criteria Evaluation is a systematic analysis of a business strategy to assess alignment with organizational interests as well as gauge effectiveness and efficiency of the business strategy under evaluation.

The strategy is evaluated based on the following:

- Consistency: the strategy must not present mutually inconsistent goals and policies
- Consonance: the strategy must represent an adaptive response to the external environment and to critical changes occurring within it
- Feasibility: the strategy must neither overtax available resources nor create unsolvable sub-problems
- Advantage: the strategy must provide for the creation and/or maintenance of a competitive advantage in the selected area of activity

According to the Rumelt's Evaluation, Costco should continue pursue the following strategies due our high evaluation scores:

- Market Penetration
- Market Development
- Product Development
- Strategic Alliance
- Horizontal Integration

According to the Rumelt's Evaluation, Costco should not move forward with following strategies due our low evaluation scores:

- Retrenchment
- Conglomerate Diversification
- Backwards Vertical Integration

Decision and Recommendation:

Corporate Strategies:

Intensive Growth Strategy: Market Penetration - Domestic

a. Increase online presence in North America to alleviate the heavy dependence on the mature warehouse club channel

b. Maintain 10% lead against primary domestic rival, Sam's Club

c. Maintain strong US geographic presence (heavy bias towards Pacific Coast)

d. Focus on building additional warehouses in Midwest and Northwest regions

e. Increase general and executive membership fees in United States, Canada, and other more established markets

f. Increase marketing through social media, internet video and still advertisements

g. Create smaller scale stores/warehouse for heavier populated areas

Intensive Growth Strategy: Market Development - International

a. Increase global reach through focusing on Asia while maintaining a modest reach in other emerging markets.

b. Pursue an ambitious expansion in more established markets (i.e. - Australia and Canada)

c. Continue to expand in Asia Pacific regions (i.e. - South Korea and Japan)

d. Pursue multi-channel reach in the UK and other European markets

Intensive Growth Strategy: Product Development

a. Maintain strong emphasis on Kirkland Signature products by creating solid brand ethos and premium warehouse positioning

b. Develop Kirkland Signature products for international locations

c. Develop more natural and/or health-conscious Kirkland signature brand options

d. Provide members with mid to high-end electronic and apparel products at deeper discounts than our competitors

Cooperative Strategy: Strategic Alliance

a. Create an online presence in China through Alibaba Group Holding Limited, which is one of the country's fastest growing online marketplace.

b. Potential partnership with Chinese e-commerce companies will help give Costco get an idea of the potential opportunities in China with low capital investments. China's online retail market is predicted to grow at an annual rate of 32.4% for the next two years ($446 billion annually)

Integrative Strategy: Horizontal Integration

a. Plan to buy out joint venture partner, Commercial Mexicana's 50% stake (totaling 32 stores) to create a stronger financial position and create a significant growth boost in Mexican market

Business Strategy:

Best-Cost Provider:

a. Secure contract with Apple to sale newly released product items for discounted prices

b. Cancel contracts with supplier whose products are selling within our allotted turnover time. Thus increasing our activity ratios

c. Test out potential partnerships with local organic farmers in the Pacific region to provide members with low cost healthier produce options

d. If successfully, implement strategy in other regions

e. Add member-only walk-in clinics to high traffic warehouses as a test run. Clinic services will able available at discounted rates and we will accept insurance

    i. We will only have Nurse Practitioners and Nurses on staff to help alleviate costs

Functional Strategies:

Information Technology

- Implement seamless system sharing between Costco and Alibaba

- Implement seamless value chain system sharing between Costco and Commercial Mexicana

- Partner with Marketing, Finance, Supply Chain, and R&D to create several IT projects for Costco mobile application creation

- Create a more user-friendly Graphical User Interface for e-commerce traffic

Human Resources

- Retain top warehouse employees are through promotional opportunities twice a year in effort to maintain top talent and have seasoned managers for new locations

- Ensure all Costco-Commercial Mexicana employees are properly trained upon acquisition

- Partner with Research & Development and Operations teams to create training sessions on new Kirkland Signature Natural and Healthy products for all Costco warehouse employees

Research & Development

- Create international and domestic teams to find locations for new general and smaller scale warehouse locations

- Obtain the necessary teams (suppliers, chemists, etc.) to create new Kirkland Signature Natural and Healthy product lines via contract

- Partner with Alibaba's e-commerce teams to get proposed products approved

- Develop business plans and review logistics for proposed warehouse clinics

Marketing

- Reach at least 10 million potential customers and potential customers monthly through social media channels (Twitter, Facebook, Tumblr, and Instagram)

- Produce six different internet commercials for potential Hulu, YouTube, Facebook, and Pandora partnerships

- Partner with Information Technology group to get new mobile application added to all mobility application stores for all major platforms (Apple, Android, etc)

Finance

- Provide Research & Development and corporate-level executives with financial analysis of each proposed warehouse location
- Provide a cost/benefit analysis of the proposed membership fee increase to corporate-level executives

Supply Chain/Operations

- Create logistics plans to implement new Kirkland Signature Natural and Healthy product lines to ensure proper visibility in each warehouse

- Place Kirkland Signature products in high traffic zones of warehouses

- Partner with Research & Development team to develop logistic plans for proposed warehouse clinics

Implementation:

Goal Number 1:

Plan to buy out joint venture partner, Commercial Mexicana's 50% stake (totaling 32 stores) to create a stronger financial position and create a significant growth boost in the Mexican market.

Participants:

The participants in in the process would include cooperation and collaboration between numerous departments as well as Costco's Executive team. Some departments include legal, finance, accounting, operations, IT, as well as store level management and store level employees. Other participants would include members of Commercial Mexicana management and their executive team as well.

Steps:

a. The executive team of Costco and the executive team of Commercial Mexicana would collaborate and negotiate an agreement that both sides would find conducive to their needs. Costco's legal team would draft contracts and legal agreements that both executive teams negotiated and agreed upon.

b. Costco Mexico would issue a dividend of $767 million. Half of the dividend would go to Costco and the other half would go to Commercial for the remainder of the 50% Costco doesn't own. Costco would then use the dividend to pay for the other half, thereby letting Costco acquire the rest of Costco Mexico.

c. Announcements would flow throw the various channels announcing the acquisition and the timeline that would associate with it.

d. Costco Mexico's CEO would remain intact, as well as staff from various departments and stores.

e. Costco would update their accounting procedures to accurately reflect the newly acquired joint venture.

f. Continue to grow their reach in Mexico's market by expanding into new regions in Mexico and develop more warehouses.

Goal Number 2:

Increase online presence in North America to alleviate heavy dependence on the mature warehouse club channel.

Participants:

The participants in in the process would include cooperation and collaboration between numerous departments such as legal, finance, accounting, operations, IT, and Marketing.

Steps:

a. Engage an Application Developer to develop a mobile application for smartphones and tablets that would create a unique user experience that would enable customers to browse, shop, and purchase products using their mobile device.

b. Decide what products would be offered and available online for members to purchase.

c. In order to entice members to try out the new mobile app, Costco would create special promotions that are only available online.

d. Promote the new mobile app and Costco's website, via marketing campaigns, designed to drive traffic to these platforms.

Bibliography

Marketline. (2014, May 12) *Costco Wholesale Corporation.* [company profile]. Retrieved from EBSCO Host database

Advantages & Disadvantages of Divisional Organizational Structure by Jason Gillikin, Demand Media

Costco Annual Report 2011-2013

Worldscope, 9/21/2013 Carrefour S.A.

Costco, Walmart, Carrefour S.A. 10-K's 2011-2013

Marketline. Global Hypermarkets & Supercenters [Industry Profile]

World Market Intelligence, Costco Wholesale Corporation Oct. 24th 2013

Crafting & Executing Strategy: The Quest for Competitive Advantage, Thompson, Peteraf, Gamble and Strickland 2014

Hoover's Company Record In-depth

http://www.euromonitor.com/costco-wholesale-corp-in-retailing/report

http://en.wikipedia.org/wiki/Market_penetration

http://en.wikipedia.org/wiki/Costco

http://yourbusiness.azcentral.com/horizontal-vs-vertical-strategic-alliances-12138.html

http://www.reuters.com/article/2014/10/14/costco-wholesale-china-idUSL3N0S93JB20141014

http://www.reuters.com/article/2012/06/14/us-costco-mexicopurchase-idUSBRE85D17V20120614

http://www.nasdaq.com/article/costco-has-room-for-growth-in-mexico-cm292002#.VHE0zRKI58U.gmail

http://www.reuters.com/article/2012/06/14/us-costco-mexicopurchase-idUSBRE85D17V20120614

http://investorplace.com/2012/06/costco-takes-control-of-its-mexico-operations/#.VHE4c-2i_pE.email

http://artcosolutions.blogspot.com/2012/06/richards-rumelt-evaluation-of-business.html

Made in the USA
Columbia, SC
14 June 2023

18033543R00044